Isaac
finds a wife

Story by Penny Frank
Illustrated by Tony Morris

CARMEL • NEW YORK 10512

The Bible tells us how God chose a special people to be his own. He made them a promise that he would always love and care for them. But they must obey him.

Abraham was chosen by God to be the first of his people. This is the story of what happened when his son Isaac needed a wife. You can find the story in your own Bible, in Genesis chapter 24.

Copyright © 1985 Lion Publishing

Published by
Lion Publishing plc
Icknield Way, Tring, Herts, England
Lion Publishing Corporation
1705 Hubbard Avenue, Batavia,
Illinois 60510, USA
Albatross Books Pty Ltd
PO Box 320, Sutherland, NSW 2232, Australia

First edition 1985
Reprinted 1987

Printed and bound in Hong Kong by Mandarin Offset
This Guideposts edition is published by special arrangement with Lion Publishing

British Library Cataloguing in Publication Data

Frank, Penny
Isaac finds a wife. – (The Lion Story Bible; 5)
1. Isaac *(Biblical patriarch)* –
Juvenile literature
2. Bible stories, English – O.T.
Genesis
I. Title   II. Series
222'.1109505   BS551.2

Library of Congress Cataloging in Publication Data

Frank, Penny.
Isaac finds a wife.
(The Lion Story Bible; 5)
1. Isaac (Biblical patriarch)—Juvenile
literature. 2. Patriarchs (Bible)—
Biography—Juvenile literature.
3. Bible. O.T.—Biography—Juvenile
literature. [1. Isaac (Biblical
patriarch) 2. Bible stories—O.T.]
I. Morris, Tony, ill. II. Title.
III. Series: Frank, Penny.
Lion Story Bible; 5.
BS580.167F7 1985   222'.1109505
84-25024

Abraham and his son Isaac lived in the
land of Canaan. Many years before,
God had promised that Abraham and his
family would live in this land. So they
had settled there and were very happy.
They trusted and loved God.
They knew God cared about them.

Abraham was very old. His wife Sarah
had died.

He said to himself, 'I must make sure
that Isaac has a wife to love him.
I don't want him to be on his own when
I die.'

4

Abraham knew that Isaac should have a wife from his own people. But they lived a long way away.

So Abraham decided to send his most trusted servant back to his home town, to find a wife for Isaac.

Abraham called his servant to him.
He was a good man. He looked after
Abraham.

'You are the person I can trust most,'
Abraham told him. 'Promise me that you
will go back to the town where my
family lives and choose a wife for Isaac
from my own people.'

The servant was worried.

'How can I make her come back with me?' he asked.

Abraham told him that God would show him what to do.

So the servant set out on the long
journey. It was hot and dusty.
The hills were steep. He had never
been that way before.

He took with him ten camels, and presents of gold, so that Abraham's family would know that the man who wanted a wife was rich.

10

At last he came to the town and rested in the shade by a well.

'Lord God,' he asked, 'please keep your promise and help me. Show me the right wife for Isaac.

'Here are some girls coming to the well for water. I will ask one of them for a drink. If she gives me one, and then offers water for my camels, I will know she is the one you have chosen.'

All the people of the town used water
from the well.

Soon a beautiful girl came to the
well. She carried a water-jar on her
shoulder.

'Please could I have a drink?' asked the servant.

   'Yes, of course,' said the girl. 'And I will give some to your thirsty camels too.'

The servant was so happy. He had
found the right wife for Isaac. He gave
her the gold rings he had in his bag.

She told him her name was Rebecca.

The servant thanked God for showing him which girl to choose.

Abraham's servant knew he must meet Rebecca's family and tell them the whole story.

'Is there somewhere I can stay for the night?' he asked Rebecca.

'Yes, there is room with my family. Come and meet them,' she said.

The servant went to Rebecca's house.
Her family were very surprised.

They saw the gold rings and heard
how God had sent the servant to choose
a wife for his master's son.

'We will miss her if she goes with you,'
they said. 'But Rebecca must decide.'

Rebecca said she would go with the
servant and be Isaac's wife.

The next day Rebecca and the servant
went back along the way to Canaan.
Rebecca took her own servant with her.

When they were near Abraham's home, Isaac came to meet them. When he saw Rebecca, he loved her and wanted her to be his wife.

'Come to meet my father Abraham and see where we live,' Isaac said.

Rebecca was glad she had been brave enough to come. Rebecca became Isaac's wife.

Isaac and Rebecca were very happy and that made Abraham happy too.

They were all glad they had trusted God to find Isaac the right wife.

The Story Bible Series from Guideposts is made up of 50 individual stories for young readers, building up an understanding of the Bible as one story—God's story—a story for all time and all people.

The Old Testament story books tell the story of a great nation—God's chosen people, the Israelites—and God's love and care for them through good times and bad. The stories are about people who knew and trusted God. From this nation came one special person, Jesus Christ, sent by God to save all people everywhere.

The New Testament story books cover the life and teaching of God's Son, Jesus. The stories are about the people he met, what he did and what he said. Almost all we know about the life of Jesus is recorded in the four Gospels—Matthew, Mark, Luke and John. The word gospel means 'good news.'

The last four stories in this section are about the first Christians, who started to tell others the 'good news,' as Jesus had commanded them—a story which continues today all over the world.

The story, *Isaac finds a wife*, comes from the first book of the Old Testament, Genesis chapter 24. God had promised Abraham that he would become the founder of a great nation. His son Isaac was born when both his parents were old, fulfilling God's promise. The matter of a wife for Isaac was vitally important. The local Canaanite girls with their own strange gods would not do. So Abraham sent his servant to northern Mesopotamia to choose a wife from his own family. The story shows how God guides in every detail.